Acknowledging GOD

Praise as a Part of Jesus' Healing

This page intentionally left blank.

Praise as a Part of Jesus' Healing

By Richard H. Ashworth

Cover design: David Berthiaume, Creative Media
Interior design: Shirley M. Bolivar

ISBN: 978-1-5136-6861-1

Dedication

With humble thanks, this book is dedicated to the Holy Spirit, who led and motivated me to record His blessings.

Acknowledgements

Earthly thanks is given to Lisa Shockey for the jump start to this project, Joy Lee for her work with dictation and transcription of the content, Shirley M. Bolivar for her copyediting and interior design, David Berthiaume of Creative Media for the cover design, and Pastor Reinhardt Stander for guidance throughout this whole process.

Last, but not least, thanks goes to my family and friends for encouragement and taunts and to the people that He draws to this book to better understand God's mercies.

This page intentionally left blank.

Table of Contents

Introduction

What does it mean to acknowledge God? It's more than a nod as you pass someone in the hallway or the well-mannered cowboy in the movies who tips his hat to the ladies. It's more complicated than that. It's when we recognize who God is and what He has done for us. In response, we place Him on the throne of our lives as Lord. It's a choice. This choice to acknowledge God is a result of the freedom God has given us to choose Him. For when we recognize what God has done for us, we will praise Him.

The Father glorifies the Son, and the Son glorifies the Father. Notice that the Father does not glorify Himself, and the Son does not glorify Himself, because God is not a self-glorifying entity. God reveals Himself to us so we can glorify Him.

This page intentionally left blank.

Background

When studying the Bible, certain patterns in wording become evident. These don't give me special insight into God, but they often make teaching others simpler. You can point out the pattern for others to see. When things are repeated in Scripture, it signifies importance to both the writer and the Holy Spirit. It's an indication to put this in your notes; it's going to be on the test. Patterns are a good way for conveying meaning to others.

While doing a study of the healing miracles of Jesus, a pattern began to emerge as to what the participants in the miracle brought to the situation. The pattern has four components. God brings (1) the power to overcome sin, cure illness, and vanquish demons as well as (2) He brings the will or desire to heal the person. First Timothy 2:4 says "who desires all men to be saved and to come to the knowledge of the truth."* Man brings (3) faith. Faith is not always the recipient's faith (it may be parental faith for a child, faith of the living for someone who has died, or faith of friends or companions, for example).

The final item in the pattern is (4) praising God in response to the miracle. Although it is not mentioned often, experience shows human nature responds when something astonishing or miraculous happens, such as at a sporting event when the big play occurs. When the baseball easily sails over the fence, it brings the crowd to its feet, fans cheering and challenging each other with, "Did you see that?" We become physically and verbally involved in the moment. The same physical and emotional response happens when one is in the presence of one of God's miracles.

While Jesus' miracles validated that He had indeed come from God, they weren't His main ministry. In addition to His goal of making salvation obtainable to sinful men, Jesus came to teach men how to live in communion with God so that through His power they might accomplish what He called them to do. Occasionally, crowds seeking healing forced Jesus to leave an area

---

* According to *The New Strong's Exhaustive Concordance of the Bible,* Thomas Nelson Publishing © 2007, *healed* and *saved* both mean "to make well, to heal, to make complete," but *saved* also goes further by including "protection."

in order to focus on His teaching. However, miracles continued throughout His ministry.

Who Touched Me?

Healing the Woman with the Issue of Blood

Based on Matthew 9:20-22; Mark 5:25-34; Luke 8:43-48

A woman who had had a hemorrhage for twelve years, and had endured much at the hands of many physicians, and had spent all that she had and was not helped at all, but rather had grown worse—after hearing about Jesus, she came up in the crowd behind *Him* and touched His cloak. For she thought, "If I just touch His garments, I will get well." Immediately the flow of her blood was dried up; and she felt in her body that she was healed of her affliction. Immediately Jesus, perceiving in Himself that the power *proceeding* from Him had gone forth, turned around in the crowd and said, "Who touched My garments?" And His disciples said to Him, "You see the crowd pressing in on You, and You say, 'Who touched Me?'" And He looked around to see the woman who had done this. But the woman fearing and trembling, aware of what had happened to her, came and fell down before Him and told Him the whole truth. And He said to her, "Daughter, your faith has made you well; go in peace and be healed of your affliction." Mark 5:25-34.

Although this may actually appear to be an intrusion in the story of Jairus getting Jesus to go heal his daughter, some believe it was included to increase Jairus' faith in Jesus' healing ability. The woman's history is interesting in that she had been dealing with this problem for 12 years and had spent a lot of money and endured much suffering at the hands of doctors. Then, she hears about Jesus. In her desperation, it occurs to her that if she just touches His cloak, she will be healed. The crowd following Jesus works to her advantage in providing anonymity, conceals her actions, and allows her to slip away unnoticed. Had she announced her unclean status, the sea of mostly Jewish men would have parted like the Red Sea before Moses. (See Leviticus 15:19-30 for an explanation of the cultural stigma.)

When she got close enough to Jesus, she touched Him, and she was healed. As she felt the change take place in her body, Jesus felt the power leave His body. And then He asked, "Who touched Me?" Touching conveys the transfer of vitality, healing, and life. In most healing situations, Jesus touched the recipient; but here, she touched Him. He didn't initiate the touch, which is why He questioned who touched Him. At first glance, it's a ridiculous question to ask in the midst of a jostling crowd. But her touch was different from the casual bumps or curious hands. Her faith that Jesus could heal her gave her access to the healing power that He had.

The word *look,* translated, means to peer intently. This describes the look of Jesus that perceives even the soul. Withering under the look, the woman fell to her knees before Jesus and confessed her situation and the healing. One of the reasons that Jesus confronted her was to offer the onlookers an opportunity to praise God for what had happened. The second reason Jesus wanted to speak to the woman was to clarify that it was her faith in Him that healed her and not the superstitious touching of His clothes. You don't need superstition when you have the supernatural Son of God standing before you.*

Where do you fall on the superstition to supernatural continuum?

* For further study, see the unusual healing situations for Jesus in Mark 3:10 and 6:56, and for the apostles in Acts 5:15 and 19:11, 12.

She's Only Sleeping

Raising Jairus' Daughter

Based on Matthew 9:18, 19, 23-26; Mark 5:22-24, 35-43; Luke 8:41, 42, 49-56

One of the synagogue officials named Jairus came up, and on seeing Him, fell at His feet and implored Him earnestly, saying, "My little daughter is at the point of death; *please* come and lay Your hands on her, so that she will get well and live." And He went off with him; . . .
While He was still speaking, they came from the *house of* the synagogue official, saying, "Your daughter has died; why trouble the Teacher anymore?" But Jesus, overhearing what was being spoken, said to the synagogue official, "Do not be afraid *any longer*, only believe." And He allowed no one to accompany Him, except Peter and James and John the brother of James. They came to the house of the synagogue official; and He saw a commotion, and *people* loudly weeping and wailing. And entering in, He said to them, "Why make a commotion and weep? The child has not died, but is asleep." They *began* laughing at Him. But putting them all out, He took along the child's father and mother and His own companions, and entered *the room* where the child was. Taking the child by the hand, He said to her, "Talitha kum!" (which translated means, "Little girl, I say to you, get up!"). Immediately the girl got up and *began* to walk, for she was twelve years old. And immediately they were completely astounded. And He gave them strict orders that no one should know about this, and He said that *something* should be given her to eat. Mark 5:22-24, 35-43.

Jairus, mentioned by name in Mark and Luke, is a synagogue official, probably at Capernaum. As an official, he functioned like a deacon, assisting the flow of the people. He wasn't a priest, performing sacrifices, but rather he took care of the secular matters pertaining to the service. From his vantage point, he may have witnessed Jesus healing people and known Jesus was the One he needed when his daughter became deathly ill. Jesus responded to his plight by agreeing to go with him.

The interruption, by the woman in the "Who Touched Me?" chapter, is seen by many as reinforcement for Jairus' faith. Seeing someone healed should fortify his faith in Jesus as a healer.

The message that he received from his house that his daughter had died was diffused by Jesus' challenge to believe in Him. And they proceeded on their way.

When they arrived at the house, they were greeted by the wailing of the paid mourners. Within the Jewish culture, funerals and burials were of great significance. They symbolized the prestige and position within the culture. Often families would hire professional mourners to express their grief. Many times these paid mourners used antiphonal responses.

When Jesus told them that the girl was just sleeping, they responded with scornful laughter. He had insulted their professionalism; they knew "dead" when they saw it. Besides, if there was no death, no one needed mourners, and they would not be paid!

Jesus' explanation that she was just sleeping is often viewed as His recognition that death was not going to be her final status, and He was going to raise her up. Jesus also used this description of sleeping when talking to His disciples about Lazarus in John 11, where Lazarus had been dead four days and thus was clearly dead.

This writer believes in a soul sleep between death and resurrection (Ecclesiastes 9:5). Following Jesus' resurrection, He told the woman in the garden not to cling to Him because He had not yet ascended to His Father (John 20:17). If anyone deserved to immediately go to heaven following death, it would be Jesus!

After Jesus had put the mourners out of the house, He took Peter,

James, John, and the girl's parents into the room where she was laid. This writer believes that Peter, James, and John were experiential learners, while other disciples could believe without firsthand experience. Jesus employed touch by taking the girl's hand and verbally commanding her, "Little girl, arise!" What power! And she awoke, arose, and walked around the room.

Following her resurrection, Jesus gave two instructions to the parents. One was to give her something to eat to prove that she was not a spirit. Second, He instructed the parents not to tell anyone about what had happened, as this news could hinder His teaching and travel.*

> How could the parents praise God for what had happened and yet tell no one about it? And you, reader, what do you believe is the condition of your soul between death and resurrection?

* For an emotional rendering from the father's point of view, access the YouTube music video of Don Francisco's "Got to Tell Somebody."

This page intentionally left blank.

All Things Are Possible

Delivering a Demon-Possessed Boy

Based on Matthew 17:14-18; Mark 9:14-29; Luke 9:38-42

When they came *back* to the disciples, they saw a large crowd around them, and *some* scribes arguing with them. Immediately, when the entire crowd saw Him, they were amazed and *began* running up to greet Him. And He asked them, "What are you discussing with them?" And one of the crowd answered Him, "Teacher, I brought You my son, possessed with a spirit which makes him mute; and whenever it seizes him, it slams him *to the ground* and he foams *at the mouth*, and grinds his teeth and stiffens out. I told Your disciples to cast it out, and they could not *do it*." And He answered them and said, "O unbelieving generation, how long shall I be with you? How long shall I put up with you? Bring him to Me!" They brought the boy to Him. When he saw Him, immediately the spirit threw him into a convulsion, and falling to the ground, he *began* rolling around and foaming *at the mouth*. And He asked his father, "How long has this been happening to him?" And he said, "From childhood. It has often thrown him both into the fire and into the water to destroy him. But if You can do anything, take pity on us and help us!" And Jesus said to him, "'If You can?' All things are possible to him who believes." Immediately the boy's father cried out and said, "I do believe; help my unbelief." When Jesus saw that a crowd was rapidly gathering, He rebuked the unclean spirit, saying to it, "You deaf and mute spirit, I command you, come out of him and do not enter him again." After crying out and throwing him into terrible convulsions, it came out; and *the boy* became so much like a corpse that most *of them* said, "He is dead!" But Jesus took him by the hand and raised him; and he got up. When He came into *the* house, His disciples *began* questioning Him privately, "Why could we not drive it out?" And He said to them, "This kind cannot come out by anything but prayer."

Mark 9:14-29.

Acknowledging God

Jesus and His three disciples, Peter, James, and John, were returning from a mountain-top experience when they noticed a crowd that included scribes and His other disciples. They seemed to be discussing something serious. When the crowd saw Jesus, they moved toward Him. Jesus inquired of His disciples as to what they were discussing with the scribes. This was protection for His disciples, for He had warned them to beware of the leaven (influence) of the misguided religious leaders. A man from the crowd told Jesus that he had brought his son to Him to be healed and that His disciples were unable to cast the demon out. The man's faith was that Jesus could heal his son. His faith did not include the disciples, which was part of the reason for their failure.

Jesus said, "Bring the boy to Me." When the boy saw Jesus, the demon threw the child into convulsions. What appears to be small talk initiated by Jesus was an opportunity for the father's faith to grow stronger. The father said, "If You can, please help us." The father's wavering faith was based on the apparent inability of anyone to heal his son. Jesus responded by repeating, "If You can?" Jesus then reassured the man that all things are possible to him who believes. The man responded with one of the most honest phrases uttered in Scripture, "I do believe; help my unbelief!" The man's belief was based on his desire for his son to be healed; his unbelief was based on the inability of anyone to heal his son so far. Whether influenced by superstition or faltering faith, Jesus meets us where we are, but He loves us too much to leave us there.

As the crowd moved toward Jesus and the boy, He commanded the unclean spirit to come out of the boy and to never re-enter him. The demon responded by essentially throwing the boy on the ground, where he lay so still that the crowd remarked, "He's dead." But Jesus, using touch to transfer vitality, healing, and life, raised the boy up!

Later, His disciples questioned why they could not cast out the demon. Jesus responded that this type of healing requires prayer and fasting. Perhaps this suggests that their lack of personal preparation while Jesus was gone weakened them in the face of so great a challenge.

Consider the seven sons of Sceva in Acts 19.

"But also some of the Jewish exorcists, who went from place to place, attempted to use the name of the Lord Jesus over those who had the evil spirits, saying, 'I order you in the name of Jesus whom Paul preaches!' Now there were seven sons of Sceva, a Jewish chief priest, doing this. But the evil spirit responded and said to them, 'I recognize Jesus, and I know of Paul, but who are you?' And the man in whom was the evil spirit, pounced on them and subdued all of them and overpowered them, so that they fled out of that house naked and wounded." Acts 19:13-16.

This example reflects being unprepared to meet this kind of spirit.

How do you deal with your lack of faith?

Jesus Talking Like a Jew

Delivering a Syrophoenician's Daughter

Based on Matthew 15:21-28; Mark 7:24-30

Jesus went away from there, and withdrew into the district of Tyre and Sidon. And a Canaanite woman from that region came out and began to cry out, saying, "Have mercy on me, Lord, Son of David; my daughter is cruelly demon-possessed." But He did not answer her a word. And His disciples came and implored Him, saying, "Send her away, because she keeps shouting at us." But He answered and said, "I was sent only to the lost sheep of the house of Israel." But she came and *began* to bow down before Him, saying, "Lord, help me!" And He answered and said, "It is not good to take the children's bread and throw it to the dogs." But she said, "Yes, Lord; but even the dogs feed on the crumbs which fall from their masters' table." Then Jesus said to her, "O woman, your faith is great; it shall be done for you as you wish." And her daughter was healed at once. Matthew 15:21-28.

In order to get some private teaching time with His disciples, Jesus left Galilee and headed to Phoenicia, which is the coastal area of the Mediterranean Sea around Tyre and Sidon. There would be fewer Jewish religious leader interruptions in this location, and they could avoid the questioning of the Jewish leaders regarding such things as eating with ceremonially unclean hands.

When they arrived in the area, they were met by a Canaanite/Gentile woman who had heard of Jesus' healing power and had come seeking His healing intervention for her demon-possessed daughter. Her approach was well-suited as she bowed down and called Jesus

"Lord" and "Son of David." She understood Jesus to be the Jewish Messiah. Tyre was 35 miles from Galilee, and Sidon was 60 miles from Galilee, yet she had heard about Him. Despite Jesus ignoring her pleas at first, she continued to beg Him to have mercy on her.

Jesus explained that He had come for the lost sheep of the house of Israel. Jesus said, "It is not good to take the bread from the children and toss it to the dog." Jesus used a word that meant a puppy as part of the household, not the term for adult or wild dogs. The woman cleverly played into this thought and said, "Even the puppies rely on the crumbs that fall from the master's table."

Instead of food, think of the "bread" as time and energy to be spent with His disciples (the children). She was not asking Him to break away from the teaching of His disciples, but just to toss her a crumb of healing mercy for her daughter.

Jesus rewarded her faithful persistence and told her that it would be done for her as she wished. The book of Mark tells us she returns home to find her daughter delivered from the demon. In retrospect, it appears that Jesus' talking like a Jew was a test of her faith by His crossing the culture lines to benefit her. Perhaps this lesson was to teach His disciples about the persistent pursuit of God's mercy.

Do you believe this woman praised God for what had happened? Did she even know whom to praise? Did she return to her source of information and report her experience? Does it ever seem that Jesus is ignoring your pleas for mercy? What is He trying to teach you?

Do You Want to Be Healed?

Healing a Lame Man at the Pool of Bethesda
Based on John 5:1-16

After these things there was a feast of the Jews, and Jesus went up to Jerusalem.
Now there is in Jerusalem by the sheep gate a pool, which is called in Hebrew Bethesda, having five porticoes. In these lay a multitude of those who were sick, blind, lame, and withered, waiting for the moving of the waters; for an angel of the Lord went down at certain seasons into the pool and stirred up the water; whoever then first, after the stirring up of the water, stepped in was made well from whatever disease with which he was afflicted. A man was there who had been ill for thirty-eight years. When Jesus saw him lying *there,* and knew that he had already been a long time *in that condition,* He said to him, "Do you wish to get well?" The sick man answered Him, "Sir, I have no man to put me into the pool when the water is stirred up, but while I am coming, another steps down before me." Jesus said to him, "Get up, pick up your pallet and walk." Immediately the man became well, and picked up his pallet and *began* to walk. Now it was the Sabbath on that day. So the Jews were saying to the man who was cured, "It is the Sabbath, and it is not permissible for you to carry your pallet." But he answered them, "He who made me well was the one who said to me, 'Pick up your pallet and walk.'" They asked him, "Who is the man who said to you, 'Pick up *your pallet* and walk'?" But the man who was healed did not know who it was, for Jesus had slipped away while there was a crowd in *that* place. Afterward Jesus found him in the temple and said to him, "Behold, you have become well; do not sin anymore, so that nothing worse happens to you." The man went away, and told the Jews that it was Jesus who had made him well. For this reason the Jews were persecuting Jesus, because He was doing these things on the Sabbath. John 5:1-16.

Acknowledging God

This author attended a small church with a medical doctor/anesthesiologist who would travel to poor Caribbean islands with a surgical team annually to perform no-cost surgeries for the island inhabitants. One of their specialties was repairing cleft palates. During one trip, they performed a cleft palate repair surgery on a young adult man who had made his living to that point by begging for money. With his surgical repair, the man lost his ability to continue begging. With no visible disability, people would not donate to his begging. When the surgical team returned to the island the next year, the man approached the doctors telling them that since they had taken away his qualifications to beg, they should support him now.

With this incident as a background, the question Jesus asked makes a lot of sense. Had the young man in the above example known the end from the beginning, he may have chosen not to have surgery. In our biblical example, the man offered explanations for his circumstances that kept him from being able to capitalize on the alleged superstitious benefits of the pool being stirred up. The verses that describe an angel stirring the waters to bring about a miracle are not included in any manuscripts prior to AD 400.*

Why had Jesus selected this man to be healed? Was it because of his lengthy known history of disability (38 years)? The length of time this man had been disabled made his case seem hopeless. It becomes obvious that the man did not know Jesus or who He was, and had expressed no faith—yet.

In a series of commands, Jesus ordered the man to stand up, take up his bed, and walk—all things he was unable to do to this point.

---

* According to *Bible Knowledge Commentary: Old and New Testament,* by Roy Zuck and John Walvoord; David C. Cook, publisher © 1989.

The authority of Jesus' commands sparked faith within the man to respond. The man demonstrated the faith he had not verbalized by doing what Jesus had told him to do.

The Bible notes that his healing took place on the Sabbath. Many times Jesus would perform miracles on the Sabbath to challenge the Jews about their burdensome rules and to educate them that the Messiah was Lord of the Sabbath.

When the Jews challenged the healed man about carrying his pallet on the Sabbath, he again sidestepped responsibility by saying, "The Man who healed me told me to carry it." How could he have refused the command of the person who healed him, he reasoned.

When Jesus found the man in the temple, He warned him against sinning, as spiritual paralysis would be worse than the physical paralysis he had suffered. This does not prove that his physical illness was the result of sin; just that Jesus desired the man to be saved as well as healed.

The man then went to the Jewish leaders and identified Jesus as the One who had healed him and told him to carry his bed. After 38 years on the bottom of the social hierarchy, this man suddenly had something the powerful people wanted. This was too great an opportunity for him to pass up.

The religious leaders disliked Jesus breaking their Sabbath rules, and they hated Him for calling God His Father, which indicated equality between God and Jesus. Because of this blasphemy, the religious leaders began thinking about the need to kill Jesus.

Do you know anyone who always has an excuse or explanation as to why their current situation is never their fault? This is a common response of people involved in the court systems.

It is interesting that the superstitious belief about the waters being stirred by an angel attributes the action to God. But the superstition, like most, appears to be of the devil, meant to discourage people who just miss the alleged awards that never seem to really happen. To cause doubt has been one of Satan's tricks from the very beginning.

Acknowledging God

When you face doubt, recognize the source, and run to Jesus.

Can you think of any current religious superstitions that may also give an unbiblical look at God? (Purgatory?)

The Blind Man Who Saw Messiah

Jesus Heals a Man Born Blind; the Response of the Jews
Based on John 9:1-38

As He passed by, He saw a man blind from birth. And His disciples asked Him, "Rabbi, who sinned, this man or his parents, that he would be born blind?" Jesus answered, *"It was* neither *that* this man sinned, nor his parents; but *it was* so that the works of God might be displayed in him. We must work the works of Him who sent Me as long as it is day; night is coming when no one can work. While I am in the world, I am the Light of the world." When He had said this, He spat on the ground, and made clay of the spittle, and applied the clay to his eyes, and said to him, "Go, wash in the pool of Siloam" (which is translated, Sent). So he went away and washed, and came *back* seeing. Therefore the neighbors, and those who previously saw him as a beggar, were saying, "Is not this the one who used to sit and beg?" Others were saying, "This is he," *still* others were saying, "No, but he is like him." He kept saying, "I am the one." So they were saying to him, "How then were your eyes opened?" He answered, "The man who is called Jesus made clay, and anointed my eyes, and said to me, 'Go to Siloam and wash'; so I went away and washed, and I received sight." They said to him, "Where is He?" He said, "I do not know."

Controversy over the Man

They brought to the Pharisees the man who was formerly blind. Now it was a Sabbath on the day when Jesus made the clay and opened his eyes. Then the Pharisees also were asking him again how he received his sight. And he said to them, "He applied clay to my eyes, and I washed, and I see." Therefore some of the Pharisees were saying, "This man is not from God, because He does not keep the Sabbath." But others were saying, "How can a man who is a sinner perform such signs?" And there was a division among them. So they said to the blind man

again, "What do you say about Him, since He opened your eyes?" And he said, "He is a prophet."
The Jews then did not believe *it* of him, that he had been blind and had received sight, until they called the parents of the very one who had received his sight, and questioned them, saying, "Is this your son, who you say was born blind? Then how does he now see?" His parents answered them and said, "We know that this is our son, and that he was born blind; but how he now sees, we do not know; or who opened his eyes, we do not know. Ask him; he is of age, he will speak for himself." His parents said this because they were afraid of the Jews; for the Jews had already agreed that if anyone confessed Him to be Christ, he was to be put out of the synagogue. For this reason his parents said, "He is of age; ask him."
So a second time they called the man who had been blind, and said to him, "Give glory to God; we know that this man is a sinner." He then answered, "Whether He is a sinner, I do not know; one thing I do know, that though I was blind, now I see." So they said to him, "What did He do to you? How did He open your eyes?" He answered them, "I told you already and you did not listen; why do you want to hear *it* again? You do not want to become His disciples too, do you?" They reviled him and said, "You are His disciple, but we are disciples of Moses. We know that God has spoken to Moses, but as for this man, we do not know where He is from." The man answered and said to them, "Well, here is an amazing thing, that you do not know where He is from, and *yet* He opened my eyes. We know that God does not hear sinners; but if anyone is God-fearing and does His will, He hears him. Since the beginning of time it has never been heard that anyone opened the eyes of a person born blind. If this man were not from God, He could do nothing." They answered him, "You were born entirely in sins, and are you teaching us?" So they put him out.

Jesus Affirms His Deity

Jesus heard that they had put him out, and finding him, He said,

The Blind Man Who Saw Messiah

"Do you believe in the Son of Man?" He answered, "Who is He, Lord, that I may believe in Him?" Jesus said to him, "You have both seen Him, and He is the one who is talking with you." And he said, "Lord, I believe." And he worshiped Him. John 9:1-38.

Common thought was that disease and disability were the result of sin in a person's life (remember Job's friends?). A baby born blind raises the question of who had sinned to bring about this disability. Can a baby in the womb sin? Or was this the result of the parents' sin? The disciples wanted to know (see Ezekiel 18).

Jesus clarified that not all disabilities are the result of sin in the person's life. His explanation does not suggest that God permitted the blindness of a baby to glorify His Son in the future; rather, Jesus' explanation meant that God would be glorified through correcting this judgmental view.

Jesus spoke of doing the will of the One who sent Him while it is still day, for the night is coming. The night represents His death. It is also interesting that He referred to Himself as the Light of the World by opening the eyes of a blind man.

Jesus' interaction with each of the miracle recipients was based on their understanding of what a healer would do. Jesus spit on the ground and made a clay mixture and placed it on the man's eyes. Kneading clay was forbidden by the Jewish religious leaders as excessive work on the Sabbath. This was another burdensome Jewish rule placed on the Sabbath. Jesus then told the man to go wash in the pool of Siloam. The name means "sent" and probably reflects this miracle as Jesus sent this man to the pool.

Upon washing his eyes, he could see. Imagine the excitement

and wonder of all those new things he saw! When the man returned seeing, it caused discussion among the people who knew him as the blind beggar—as to whether it was him or someone else. When the people heard his explanation of being healed, they took him to the Pharisees to interpret their understanding of what had happened.

As the Pharisees considered Jesus to be a sinner for breaking one of their Sabbath restrictions of making clay, they set out to deny the miracle or discredit Jesus. The Pharisees even brought in the blind man's parents to try to deny that the man had been born blind, which would then deny the healing. The parents were fearful, for they knew that the Pharisees would cast anyone out of the synagogue who supported Jesus. The blind man engaged in lively banter with the Pharisees about what had happened to him and the miracle at the hand of Jesus. The Pharisees questioned the man three times about what had happened, hoping to catch him in a contradiction. But, the man held true to what had happened to him. When the man finally asked the Pharisees if he needed to repeat the story because they wanted to become disciples of Jesus, their injured pride caused them to insult the man and throw him out of the synagogue.

After hearing that the man had been put out of the synagogue, Jesus found him and asked him if he believed in Messiah. The man, who had not seen Jesus, said he did and asked who Messiah was. Jesus identified Himself as Messiah, and the man worshipped Him! The man received his sight and a vision of his future through salvation.

Which would thrill you more?

The Synagogue

The synagogue, which means "assembly" or "meeting," was developed by the Jews during their Babylonian captivity to study the Scriptures and to determine how they ended up in captivity. Their purpose in studying the Scriptures was to determine what they had done against God that led to them getting carried off. Several new patterns were implemented upon their return to Judah to purify their religious and cultural practices. The concept of the synagogue remained with the Jewish people and formed the backbone of their religious practices and Sabbath services. The temple was rebuilt and continued to be used for offerings in Jerusalem. Synagogues were also located in many cities and served particular groups in the large cities, such as the Greek-speaking synagogue in Jerusalem.

To gain an understanding of the worship service, one can review Luke 4:16-30.

The people in Nazareth had heard about Jesus' ministry and the miracles that He had performed in Capernaum. This became obvious in the exchange that took place in the synagogue. As a visiting teacher, Jesus was given the scroll containing the book of Isaiah, and He opened it to what we call chapter 61 beginning at verse one. The reader would stand while he read the Scripture, then would sit down for commentary and discussion. So Jesus read, "The Spirit of the Lord is upon Me, Because He anointed Me to preach the gospel to the poor. He has sent Me to proclaim release to the captives, And recovery of sight to the blind, To set free those who are oppressed, To proclaim the favorable year of the Lord" (Luke 4:18, 19). It must be noted that Jesus stopped reading just before Isaiah spoke of judgment on his people, because that will occur at Jesus' second coming. Jesus then sat down and said, "Today this Scripture has been fulfilled in your hearing."

The word *anointed* has two meanings: 1) to smear with oil, and 2) to consecrate one to a task or a religion.*

To this point every eye was on Him, and all spoke well of Him. Problems arose when the people questioned Him about doing the same miracles in Nazareth that He had done in other places. His response angered the people as He reviewed the history of the Jews during Elijah's time when there were many widows, but only the

---

* *The New Strong's Exhaustive Concordance of the Bible,* Thomas Nelson Publishing © 2007.

widow in Zarephath benefitted from a miracle during the famine. Also, there were many lepers, but only Naaman was cleansed. The enraging part of His message was that these recipients of great miracles were Gentiles, suggesting that the Gentiles would receive miracles before the people of Nazareth would. He explained that a prophet has no honor in his hometown—meaning, no people of faith to support the miracles.

The crowd's anger grew to rage, and they pushed Him out of the synagogue toward the side of the cliff on which their city sat. However, Jesus walked through their midst and went His way. While mob violence was not a part of the pattern of worship, Jesus' presence and comments often enraged the religious leaders who considered themselves to be the authority on religious matters.

The Honor and Shame Culture

The American culture is based on guilt and innocence and is reflected in our courts and judicial systems.

Within the Middle East, the culture balances between shame and honor. It is a closed system in which one can only increase his honor by increasing his opponent's shame. This can be seen readily in the interactions between Jesus and the religious leaders. In the story of the man born blind, the Pharisees challenged the healed man with whether he was ever truly blind, but also that Jesus was a sinner because He broke one of the Pharisees' limitations on Sabbath work. As the conversation continued and the former blind man challenged them, questioning if they wanted to be Jesus' disciples, they heaped shame on him, because his blindness must have been caused from being born in sin. They then threw him out of the synagogue, which would severely limit his access for worship. If one were denied access to the temple, he would lose access to God, so this was quite a serious matter.

That is why Jesus sought the man out and challenged him if he believed in the Messiah. The man replied, "Sir, who is he, that I may believe?" When Jesus explained who He was, the blind man worshipped Him. What a wonderful ending to this story!

In the conversation with the woman at the well, Jesus told her that a time was coming when men would worship God in spirit and not in earthly temples (John 4:21-23).

The shame/honor context still exists in Middle Eastern countries and is one of the difficulties Christians must overcome when sharing the gospel with a Middle Eastern person. The isolation of shame keeps many from accepting Christianity.*

---

* For additional information on the shame/honor culture, contact Ravi Zacharias International Ministry (rzim.org), or read *Seeing Jesus Through Middle Eastern Eyes: Cultural Studies in the Gospels,* by Kenneth E. Bailey; published by SPCK © 2008.

Choose Your Friends Wisely

Healing a Paralytic

Based on Matthew 9:2-8; Mark 2:3-12; Luke 5:18-26

And *some* men *were* carrying on a bed a man who was paralyzed; and they were trying to bring him in and to set him down in front of Him. But not finding any *way* to bring him in because of the crowd, they went up on the roof and let him down through the tiles with his stretcher, into the middle *of the crowd,* in front of Jesus. Seeing their faith, He said, Friend, your sins are forgiven you." The scribes and the Pharisees began to reason, saying, "Who is this *man* who speaks blasphemies? Who can forgive sins, but God alone?" But Jesus, aware of their reasonings, answered and said to them, "Why are you reasoning in your hearts? Which is easier, to say, 'Your sins have been forgiven you,' or to say, 'Get up and walk'? But, so that you may know that the Son of Man has authority on earth to forgive sins,"—He said to the paralytic—"I say to you, get up, and pick up your stretcher and go home." Immediately he got up before them, and picked up what he had been lying on, and went home glorifying God. They were all struck with astonishment and *began* glorifying God; and they were filled with fear, saying, "We have seen remarkable things today." Luke 5:18-26.

As this story opens, Jesus was sitting in a house full of people who had come to hear Him, including some scribes and Pharisees. The Bible tells us that the power of the Spirit was upon Him for healing. The word, power, used here is the Greek word *dunamis,* which indicates explosive power and is where English gets its word "dynamite."

Some men arrived carrying a paralytic on a stretcher. However, they were unable to enter the house because of the crowd. Like most homes in that area, there was an outside permanent staircase to the roof. Sometimes tents or rooms were built on the roof as needed. The men determined that since they could not enter the house through normal means, they would remove roof tiles, dig through the remaining material, and create a hole through which they could lower the paralytic down into the house right in front of Jesus. Jesus recognized the faith of the friends who had brought the paralytic to His attention. Their faith was sufficient to allow for the healing.

Jesus, overlooking the problems of the man, dealt with his spiritual needs first by telling him his sins were forgiven. The scribes and Pharisees were thinking this to be a blasphemous statement, for they knew only God can forgive sins. Knowing their thoughts, Jesus asked why they were thinking that in their hearts and challenged them with this question, "Which is easier: to say, 'Your sins are forgiven' or to say, 'Take up your bed and walk?' " Obviously, it's easier to say "Your sins are forgiven" because there is no physical proof that it has occurred, while healing requires visible changes. Jesus was teaching all present that Messiah had the power to forgive sins, which was far beyond their understanding of Messiah's ministry. They expected Messiah to be a great warrior to re-establish Judah as the reigning power in the area.

In our lives, there are many things in our past that we would like to alter. However, all we can do is put our past on the altar of God's forgiveness.

Then Jesus commanded him to, "Get up, take your mat, and go home." The miraculous healing was a sign that Jesus had the power to heal and the authority to forgive sins.

The man did as Jesus had commanded: he arose, took up his bed, and went toward his home, to the amazement of everyone in the house. Both the paralytic and the many witnesses praised God for the miraculous thing they had seen that day, glorifying God for His mercy and power.

What would you say to glorify God?

This page intentionally left blank.

An Attitude of Gratitude

Jesus Heals Ten Lepers

Based on Luke 17:11-19

While He was on the way to Jerusalem, He was passing between Samaria and Galilee. As He entered a village, ten leprous men who stood at a distance met Him; and they raised their voices, saying, "Jesus, Master, have mercy on us!" When He saw them, He said to them, "Go and show yourselves to the priests." And as they were going, they were cleansed. Now one of them, when he saw that he had been healed, turned back, glorifying God with a loud voice, and he fell on his face at His feet, giving thanks to Him. And he was a Samaritan. Then Jesus answered and said, "Were there not ten cleansed? But the nine—where are they? Was no one found who returned to give glory to God, except this foreigner?" And He said to him, "Stand up and go; your faith has made you well." Luke 17:11-19.

On His way to Jerusalem, Jesus passed through an area between Galilee and Samaria. As He entered a small village, 10 leprous men recognized Him and called to Him, saying, "Jesus, have mercy on us!" Lepers had to stand away from unaffected people and proclaim their disgrace by announcing, "Unclean!" When Jesus saw them, He told them, "Go present yourselves to the priests."

As they began to obey Jesus' command, they were healed of their leprosy. Upon seeing that he was healed, one man turned back praising God, and bowed his face to the ground before Jesus. The Bible notes that this man was a Samaritan.

Historically, when the Assyrians overran the northern kingdom called Israel in 721 BC, they carried off everyone except the very poor nomadic herdsmen. These Jews intermarried with Assyrians who moved into the area and thus polluted their religious beliefs with the pagans. Following Cyrus the Persian's decree in 538 BC that the Jews could return to Judah—the southern kingdom—from their Babylonian captivity, they wanted nothing to do with the half-breed descendants they called Samaritans.

Jesus noted that the only one of the 10 who returned was a foreigner. Many commentators believe that this action of the Jewish lepers reflected the Jewish people's rejection of Jesus as the Messiah.

It should be noted that the Jews were doing what Jesus had told them to do, to present themselves before the priests, to be certified as cleansed from leprosy (see Leviticus 14:1-30). Jesus had also accused the Pharisees of following the laws but missing the weightier matters of kindness, relationships, and gratitude.

It is interesting to note that their shared ostracism from their culture allowed them to mingle with a leprous Samaritan. It seemed that their shared misery trumped their prejudices. After being cleansed and certified by the priests, they could return to the community and their mistrust of Samaritans.

Jesus told the man that his faith had made him well and to go his way. Samaritans did expect a Moses-like Messiah to come, and this Samaritan was so blessed that he saw Jesus as the Messiah.

How serious a crisis would it take for you to overcome your prejudices?

Jesus, Legion, and the Pigs

Delivering the Gadarene Demoniac

Based on Matthew 8:28-34; Mark 5:1-20; Luke 8:26-39

They came to the other side of the sea, into the country of the Gerasenes. When He got out of the boat, immediately a man from the tombs with an unclean spirit met Him, and he had his dwelling among the tombs. And no one was able to bind him anymore, even with a chain; because he had often been bound with shackles and chains, and the chains had been torn apart by him and the shackles broken in pieces, and no one was strong enough to subdue him. Constantly, night and day, he was screaming among the tombs and in the mountains, and gashing himself with stones. Seeing Jesus from a distance, he ran up and bowed down before Him; and shouting with a loud voice, he said, "What business do we have with each other, Jesus, Son of the Most High God? I implore You by God, do not torment me!" For He had been saying to him, "Come out of the man, you unclean spirit!" And He was asking him, "What is your name?" And he said to Him, "My name is Legion; for we are many." And he *began* to implore Him earnestly not to send them out of the country. Now there was a large herd of swine feeding nearby on the mountain. *The demons* implored Him, saying, "Send us into the swine so that we may enter them." Jesus gave them permission. And coming out, the unclean spirits entered the swine; and the herd rushed down the steep bank into the sea, about two thousand *of them;* and they were drowned in the sea.

Their herdsmen ran away and reported it in the city and in the country. And *the people* came to see what it was that had happened. They came to Jesus and observed the man who had been demon-possessed sitting down, clothed and in his right mind, the very man who had had the "legion"; and they became frightened. Those who had seen it described to them how it had happened to the demon-possessed man, and *all* about the swine. And they began to implore Him to leave their region. As

Acknowledging God

He was getting into the boat, the man who had been demon-possessed was imploring Him that he might accompany Him. And He did not let him, but He said to him, "Go home to your people and report to them what great things the Lord has done for you, and *how* He had mercy on you." And he went away and began to proclaim in Decapolis what great things Jesus had done for him; and everyone was amazed. Mark 5:1-20.

Jesus and His disciples crossed the Sea of Galilee and landed at a Gentile area on the southeastern shore of the lake. The three gospels that contain this story vary in identifying the closest town of 10 that made up the Decapolis. The villages of Gennesaret and Gedara are the two closest to the lake, which some Gentile maps call the Sea of Gennesaret.

As soon as Jesus steps out of the boat, He is approached by a demon-possessed man who had quite a reputation among the folks who lived there. Showing amazing strength, the demon-possessed man could not be bound, not even with chains and fetters, which he would break. He would cry out both day and night, would gash himself with stones, and made passing by the tombs challenging to everyone. In Matthew, there are two possessed men, but one of them is the dominant spirit that engages Jesus.

It is interesting that the demon recognized Jesus as the Son of the Most High God, while many people were uncertain. This name was often used by Gentiles who did not know God in the Old Testament. This may also have been an attempt to gain power over Jesus by calling His name, a common practice in demon worship and manipulation.

Another interesting point is how the demon questioned Jesus, like: "What business do you have with us?" and "Have You come to torment me before the time?" In answer to Jesus' question, "What is your name?" the demon replied, "Legion, for we are many." A legion was a Roman army unit of three to six thousand men, but may indicate "many" instead of an exact number. Like most legions, one demon was in control.

Note that the demon bowing his knee before Jesus does not indicate worship, but the recognition of a superior spiritual being in Jesus. Fearful of being cast into the abyss or left as a free-ranging spirit, the demon asked Jesus' permission for them to enter a herd of swine feeding on a nearby hill. Jesus permitted them to enter the pigs, and they came out of the man and entered the swine.

Apparently, for a spirit, entering swine is a lot like the first time you ride a motorcycle—they are hard to control! The pigs responded to the uninvited guests by preferring to end their lives by stampeding down the hill into the lake where the herd of 2,000 drowned.

The herdsman immediately ran to the nearby town to report what had happened, as he knew he could be held responsible for the lost animals. When the people arrived from the town, they saw the demon-possessed man clothed and in his right mind. But, they were more concerned about the economics of the afternoon's activities, and fearing additional difficulties, begged Jesus to leave their region. As Jesus prepared to honor their wishes, the man who had been cleansed begged to leave with Him and to remain in Jesus' presence. But Jesus denied his request and told him to return to his people (family) and tell them all that the Lord had done and the mercies he had received that day. The man went forth proclaiming what God had done for him. What a witness!

In spite of the names and number differences, this is a stunning story of redemption and possibilities. The former demoniac returned to his people as Jesus had told him to do and helped prepare them for accepting Jesus when He returned. (See when Jesus returned to Decapolis in Mark 7:31-37 and the feeding of the 4,000 Gentiles in Mark 8:1-9.)

Acknowledging God

Would the demoniac's story pique your curiosity to go hear Jesus?

Where There's a Will

Jesus Heals a Leper

Based on Matthew 8:2-4; Mark 1:40-45; Luke 5:12-16

And a leper came to Jesus, beseeching Him and falling on his knees before Him, and saying, "If You are willing, You can make me clean." Moved with compassion, Jesus stretched out His hand and touched him, and said to him, "I am willing; be cleansed." Immediately the leprosy left him and he was cleansed. And He sternly warned him and immediately sent him away, and He said to him, "See that you say nothing to anyone; but go, show yourself to the priest and offer for your cleansing what Moses commanded, as a testimony to them." But he went out and began to proclaim it freely and to spread the news around, to such an extent that Jesus could no longer publicly enter a city, but stayed out in unpopulated areas; and they were coming to Him from everywhere. Mark 1:40-45.

This is the only healing miracle where God's will is announced, although God's will is present in all His miracles. God's will is His willingness to participate with man in a healing process. God's will is often translated as His desire: in it is God's will or desire that all men be saved (1 Timothy 2:4).

Oftentimes we ask that our prayers be within God's will. This is our way of not forcing God's hand.

Tony Evans, pastor of a large church in Dallas and frequent radio speaker, tells of an experience where he and several other pastors were leading an evangelistic effort in an open stadium when a violent storm was reported to be heading their way. Each of the pastors prayed that the storm would miss them, and each added "if it is in Your will."

One little lady in the leadership asked if she could pray. She prayed that God had to intervene for them to do what God had called them to do in this evangelistic meeting. She was quite forceful in telling God what He needed to do. The violent storm came just as the evangelistic meeting was to begin. The storm split and went around the stadium with great torrents of rain falling on the cars in the parking lot, but not a drop fell inside the stadium. Pastor Evans believes it was because of the little woman's prayer that the storm went around the stadium. The evangelistic program was a big success with this miracle of God emphasizing His presence.

In this healing, a leprous man approached Jesus and bowed himself down before Him, saying, "If You are willing, You can make me clean." The man did not question Jesus' power to heal him. Jesus' response was to touch the man, showing that Messiah is not subject to contagious disease, and, He said, "I am willing. Be cleansed." This was the first healing of a leper since Miriam and Naaman in the Old Testament.

Jesus sternly warned the man to say nothing to anyone, but to go show himself to the priest and to make the appropriate sacrifice. The warning not to speak to anyone may have been temporary until he showed himself to the priest and was declared clean. Or, it may have been to avoid crowds of miracle-seekers who might interfere with His teaching. Either way, the man went forth proclaiming what had happened to him. The crowds clamoring for healing forced Jesus into less-populated areas to teach.

How could you not proclaim the life-altering miracle that Jesus had performed for the man? When the once leprous man returned to his people, surely they would have proclaimed the miracle to those they would meet. And what does it mean to you to be in God's will?

The Good Roman

Healing a Centurion's Servant

Based on Matthew 8:5-13; Luke 7:1-10

When He had completed all His discourse in the hearing of the people, He went to Capernaum. And a centurion's slave, who was highly regarded by him, was sick and about to die. When he heard about Jesus, he sent some Jewish elders asking Him to come and save the life of his slave. When they came to Jesus, they earnestly implored Him, saying, "He is worthy for You to grant this to him; for he loves our nation and it was he who built us our synagogue." Now Jesus *started* on His way with them; and when He was not far from the house, the centurion sent friends, saying to Him, "Lord, do not trouble Yourself further, for I am not worthy for You to come under my roof; for this reason I did not even consider myself worthy to come to You, but *just* say the word, and my servant will be healed. For I also am a man placed under authority, with soldiers under me; and I say to this one, 'Go!' and he goes, and to another, 'Come!' and he comes, and to my slave, 'Do this!' and he does it." Now when Jesus heard this, He marveled at him, and turned and said to the crowd that was following Him, "I say to you, not even in Israel have I found such great faith." When those who had been sent returned to the house, they found the slave in good health. Luke 7:1-10.

The major difference between Matthew's account and Luke's is the proximity of the main character of the centurion. Luke reports that a Roman centurion sent people to represent him to Jesus, while Matthew reports a personal exchange between Jesus and the centurion. Culturally, anyone who was sent by a person was considered the same as speaking directly to the person. This cultural understanding benefited the apostles when Jesus sent them out. This encounter occurred in Capernaum where Jesus spent a lot of time and performed many miracles.

Wisely, the Roman centurion had sent Jewish elders to present his request to Jesus, believing that a Jewish rabbi would not respond to a Roman soldier. The centurion was concerned about his servant who was sick unto death, and he believed Jesus could heal his servant. These men counted the centurion worthy of Jesus' attention, noting that the centurion had built a synagogue for them in Capernaum. No doubt Jesus had visited this very same synagogue while in that city. The Jewish envoys considered this foreigner to be a friend of the Jewish people and noted several ways he had benefited the Jews in that area.

Jesus agreed to go with them, and they started on their way. Still quite a distance from the centurion's house, the centurion sent yet another messenger to meet Jesus and tell Jesus that he was unworthy for Jesus to be in his home. Noting that he also was a man of authority, he recited how he could order soldiers or slaves to go and do his bidding. He recognized that Jesus also had this kind of authority, and as he was unworthy to entertain Jesus, he believed that Jesus could heal his servant from a distance and did not have to apply personal touch in order to accomplish this.

At this point, Jesus praised the Roman centurion's faith and lamented that such faith was scarce among the Jews. Jesus stated that strangers would come from afar and be in the heavenly kingdom with the Jewish founding fathers before many of the Jews.

When the messengers returned to the centurion's house, they found that the servant had been healed because of this foreigner's faith in Jesus. Living in Capernaum, and being a friend to the Jews, the centurion had probably heard the many stories of Jesus and His wonders in that city. He had heard enough to develop a faith sufficient to bring about the healing.

Most healings today do not require a physical touch but are often spiritually delivered. Does this require a greater or lesser faith than a direct touch?

This page intentionally left blank.

Whose Faith?

Raising a Widow's Son
Based on Luke 7:11-17

Soon afterwards He went to a city called Nain; and His disciples were going along with Him, accompanied by a large crowd. Now as He approached the gate of the city, a dead man was being carried out, the only son of his mother, and she was a widow; and a sizeable crowd from the city was with her. When the Lord saw her, He felt compassion for her, and said to her, "Do not weep." And He came up and touched the coffin; and the bearers came to a halt. And He said, "Young man, I say to you, arise!" The dead man sat up and began to speak. And *Jesus* gave him back to his mother. Fear gripped them all, and they *began* glorifying God, saying, "A great prophet has arisen among us!" and, "God has visited His people!" This report concerning Him went out all over Judea and in all the surrounding district. Luke 7:11-17.

The village of Nain is located about 25 miles southwest of Capernaum, more than a casual walk. As Jesus, His disciples, and a crowd of followers were approaching the gate of Nain, a funeral procession was coming out of the city on its tragic mission of burying a young man, the only son of a widowed woman. This would leave the widow with no close male relatives and could make her vulnerable. Although Nain was probably not Jesus' primary destination, there seemed to be a divine appointment outside the city.

There is no indication that the grieving widow was expecting

Jesus to intervene in her sorrow. The funeral procession, like the current-day processions with their little purple flags indicating "funeral," had the right of way out of respect for the departed.

Jesus felt compassion, or pity, for the widow and her situation. The word translated "compassion" is the Greek word *spachna,* which means the internal organs thought to be the center of one's emotions. Because of His pity, Jesus told the widow not to weep. Then He stepped up and put His hand on the bier, causing the bearers to halt their progress. This indicated that the crowd did not know Jesus and were not purposefully trying to intercept Him.

Jesus then said, "Young man, I say to you, arise!" The dead young man sat up and began to speak. Certainly he had a lot of questions! The Scripture then says Jesus gave the widow's son back to her.

Faith is a necessary part of any healing or resurrection. Several different sources of faith have already been explored in the healings reported so far. But whose faith carried the healing in this instance?

There was no indication of the widow having knowledge of or faith in Jesus, nor did there seem to be any recognition of Jesus among the funeral crowd. Although three of His disciples had witnessed the resurrection of Jairus' daughter, nothing in this story suggests that they had come forward or expressed faith, even after having had that experience.

Believing there are no coincidental meetings in Jesus' ministry, and based on His compassion and His close relationship with the Father, brings Jesus' faith into play in this miraculous healing. The situation required immediate intervention and did not permit time to bring other participants up to speed in their own faith.

In verses 16 and 17, the fear is awe or amazement at what had happened, and they glorified God for the miracle. The final verse in this story relates how this was communicated throughout the entire region.

Whose Faith?

Is it possible that there were people of faith who had not expressed it yet, but did after the miracle? Your salvation is a small miracle! How do you glorify God for what He has done in your life?

This page intentionally left blank.

Demons in Church?

Delivering a Synagogue Demoniac

Based on Luke 4:31-37; Mark 1:23-28; Luke 11:24-26

> And He came down to Capernaum, a city of Galilee, and He was teaching them on the Sabbath; and they were amazed at His teaching, for His message was with authority. In the synagogue there was a man possessed by the spirit of an unclean demon, and he cried out with a loud voice, "Let us alone! What business do we have with each other, Jesus of Nazareth? Have You come to destroy us? I know who You are—the Holy One of God!" But Jesus rebuked him, saying, "Be quiet and come out of him!" And when the demon had thrown him down in the midst *of the people,* he came out of him without doing him any harm. And amazement came upon them all, and they *began* talking with one another saying, "What is this message? For with authority and power He commands the unclean spirits and they come out." And the report about Him was spreading into every locality in the surrounding district. Luke 4:31-37.

On another Sabbath, in another synagogue, Jesus was teaching the people. He spoke with such authority; not like the scribes who repeated memorized answers. One of the persons present in the synagogue was a man possessed by an unclean spirit. (Did you think all the demons were in an opposing political party?) It is intriguing that the demon was in a place of study and worship, which did not seem to bother him.

The demons challenged Jesus' presence, questioning if He had come to destroy them. The demons are aware of their final destination and wondered if it was already that time. Notice that the demons always seemed to talk in a loud voice. This is a common defense of people who know that they may be facing trouble; they get loud and draw a crowd, believing that this may quiet the opposition. Nowadays, people shout down their opposition, not giving them any opportunity to speak. Note that the demons were well aware of Jesus' identity and even called Him the Holy One of God. Jesus' response to be quiet was because Jesus' goal was to be recognized as the Son of God by the people, not by the demons.

Jesus commanded the demons to come out of the man, and they had to obey. Jesus' authority amazed the people, both in His teaching, not as one who had been taught, and in His authority over unclean spirits. This was early in His ministry and was reported throughout the region.

So what do you do after the demon has left?

"When the unclean spirit goes out of a man, it passes through waterless places seeking rest, and not finding any, it says, 'I will return to my house from which I came.' And when it comes, it finds it swept and put in order. Then it goes and takes *along* seven other spirits more evil than itself, and they go in and live there; and the last state of that man becomes worse than the first" (Luke 11:24-26).

The unclean spirit described by Jesus went out looking for a new place to reside (apparently, there were no herds of swine available). Unable to find a new abode, he returned to where he had previously lived. Finding it clean but uninhabited, he decided to move back in and sought seven additional rowdy friends to live with him.

Jesus' point is that you need a more powerful spirit to move in when you have an unclean spirit leave. That spirit, of course, is God's Spirit, the Holy Spirit. The presence of God's Spirit in your life will keep the unclean spirits from establishing a foothold or returning. The presence of the Holy Spirit not only keeps out unwelcome guests, but also offers comfort, guidance, and a direct connection with God.

Can you see how vulnerable you would be without
God's Spirit dwelling in you?

Doing What They Do Best

Healing Peter's Mother-in-Law
Based on Matthew 8:14-15; Mark 1:29-31; Luke 4:38-39

Then He got up and *left* the synagogue, and entered Simon's home. Now Simon's mother-in-law was suffering from a high fever, and they asked Him to help her. And standing over her, He rebuked the fever, and it left her; and she immediately got up and waited on them. Luke 4:38, 39.

After cleansing the synagogue demoniac, Jesus and His disciples went to Simon Peter's house, where they found that his mother-in-law was suffering a high fever. Having just witnessed the cleansing of the demoniac, they asked Jesus to help her.

Jesus rebuked the fever, which only Luke, a physician, mentions. A rebuke is a command that assumes authority over what is being rebuked. A fever is the body's response to an illness or infection, so it is assumed that the rebuke included the cause of the high fever. Both the cause and the high fever left the woman, and she got up and began to serve them.

Jeremiah 29:11 says, " 'For I know the plans that I have for you,' declares the Lord, 'plans for welfare and not for calamity to give you a future and a hope.' "

Jesus did not heal the woman so that she could serve them. He healed the woman because He loves us and desires to do good for those who believe in Him. In turn, the woman got up and began to serve them, not because she was obligated, but because that is how she showed her love and appreciation for others.

At a recent Mother's Day gathering, I shared the following true story.

The Mask

At the age of 6, I would travel with my older brother and a friend to the downtown section of the city where I grew up. We would look through the Five & Dime stores, which were the only ones in our price range. Of course, we rarely had a dime. During one trip, near Halloween, I had discovered the most wonderful, full-face gorilla mask and told my mother about this fabulous treasure and how it could be purchased for $1.00. In the 1950s, my mother did not have discretionary funds of her own, and my father would never consent to such foolishness as a gorilla mask.

I don't recall my arguments, but somehow my mother was moved. She began collecting items made of metal with some weight, like a broken iron and a section of lead pipe, which we put in a two-wheeled, pull-behind grocery cart. We then pulled the cart eight blocks to a scrap metal dealer located next to the train tracks on the east side of the city. There, we sold the metal items and received a few coins.

We then walked, still pulling the empty grocery cart, an additional seven blocks to the store that held the treasure. After finding the mask, it became obvious that I had misread the price. While I do not remember how much it actually cost, I knew that our few coins would not cover it. And so we started home by a shorter route of only 12 blocks.

I did not get the mask, but I did feel loved. I wish I had conveyed that feeling to my mother that day.

Is there anyone to whom you owe a "Thank you for loving me"?

Be Like a Samaritan

Healing a Nobleman's Son at Cana
Based on John 4:46-54

Therefore He came again to Cana of Galilee where He had made the water wine. And there was a royal official whose son was sick at Capernaum. When he heard that Jesus had come out of Judea into Galilee, he went to Him and was imploring *Him* to come down and heal his son; for he was at the point of death. So Jesus said to him, "Unless you people see signs and wonders, you *simply* will not believe." The royal official said to Him, "Sir, come down before my child dies." Jesus said to him, "Go; your son lives." The man believed the word that Jesus spoke to him and started off. As he was now going down, *his* slaves met him, saying that his son was living. So he inquired of them the hour when he began to get better. Then they said to him, "Yesterday at the seventh hour the fever left him." So the father knew that *it was* at that hour in which Jesus said to him, "Your son lives"; and he himself believed and his whole household. This is again a second sign that Jesus performed when He had come out of Judea into Galilee. John 4:46-54.

Jesus had just spent two days with His disciples teaching in Samaria. The woman at the well had encountered Jesus and went to her village and piqued their curiosity about Jesus being the Promised One. The Samaritans had enough of a Jewish history to come to Jesus and hear His words. They invited Him to stay and teach them. The men of the village told the woman that they had come initially based on what she had said, but after hearing Jesus' words, they determined that He was the

Savior of the world. A personal experience with Jesus is always better than hearing about someone else's experience.

Most Jews would avoid passing through Samaria for fear of prejudicial contamination, and they would cross the Jordan River and proceed up the east side of the river, crossing the Jordan again into the Jewish territory of Galilee. Jesus always chose to walk through Samaria, allowing Godly encounters to occur.

After leaving Samaria, Jesus went to Cana where He was found by a royal officer from Capernium. The man had come 20 miles seeking Jesus, for his son was very sick. As a royal officer, the man prob-ably protected the royal interests in local happenings. Living in Capernaum, he had knowledge of Jesus as a healer and came seeking Him.

Upon his imploring Jesus to come heal his son, Jesus replied with, "Unless you people see signs and wonders, you simply will not believe." While this seems harsh, it reflects His two days of teaching in Samaria, and no one there requested a miraculous sign before they believed He was Messiah. The man was not put off by Jesus' comment and begged Him to come heal his son. Jesus' response was, "Go, your son lives." The man had sufficient faith to believe and headed home.

He was met by his slaves as he neared his home and was told that his son was well. When he asked at what hour his son began to improve, his slaves replied, "About the seventh hour." In Roman time, that would be about 7:00 pm. This was the very time when Jesus told him, "Go, your son will live." The man became a believer, and his whole household was also saved.

Since the man worked for the royal family, he was familiar with Roman time as noted above. However, as Jesus included him in the sign-seeking, unbelieving group, he was probably Jewish. Many Jews sought healing but did not acknowledge the Healer.

Do you believe in Jesus based on His words, as the Samaritans did, or do you seek signs and miracles? Is not your salvation a small miracle?

Goodness Versus Shame

Healing a Blind and Mute Demoniac

Based on Matthew 12:22; Luke 11:14-26

And He was casting out a demon, and it was mute; when the demon had gone out, the mute man spoke; and the crowds were amazed. But some of them said, "He casts out demons by Beelzebul, the ruler of the demons." Others, to test *Him,* were demanding of Him a sign from heaven. But He knew their thoughts and said to them, "Any kingdom divided against itself is laid waste; and a house divided against itself falls. If Satan also is divided against himself, how will his kingdom stand? For you say that I cast out demons by Beelzebul. And if I by Beelzebul cast out demons, by whom do your sons cast them out? So they will be your judges. But if I cast out demons by the finger of God, then the kingdom of God has come upon you. When a strong *man,* fully armed, guards his own house, his possessions are undisturbed. But when someone stronger than he attacks him and overpowers him, he takes away from him all his armor on which he had relied and distributes his plunder. He who is not with Me is against Me; and he who does not gather with Me, scatters.

"When the unclean spirit goes out of a man, it passes through waterless places seeking rest, and not finding any, it says, 'I will return to my house from which I came.' And when it comes, it finds it swept and put in order. Then it goes and takes *along* seven other spirits more evil than itself, and they go in and live there; and the last state of that man becomes worse than the first." Luke 11:14-26.

In response to His disciples' request to teach them to pray, Jesus established the pattern of what we call the

Lord's Prayer and weaved parables showing how God is a giver of good things to those who pray. The gifts that He gives are good and even His giving is good.

As our scene opens in verse 14, Jesus is doing good by healing a blind and mute demoniac (see Matthew 12:22). After casting out the demon, the man begins to see and speak. Some who were present were amazed by what had happened, but others accused Jesus of casting out demons by Beelzebul, a pagan god from the Philistine city of Ekron. The name means *lord of the high places,* as he was usually worshipped in wooded areas on mountain tops. (The Jews used the pejorative Beelzebub, which means *lord of the flies.* We all know what flies are attracted to.)

The Middle Eastern cultures are based on shame and honor in which you enhance your honor by heaping shame on another person. This was their goal: to shame Jesus by accusing Him of working for Satan instead of for God. Jesus responded to them by logically showing how a house divided against itself—Satan casting out demons—would fall. Jesus challenged them that if He was using Satan to cast out demons, then what power were their sons using to cast out demons (Acts 19:13-16)? Jesus also challenged them that if He was acting under the finger (power) of God, then the kingdom of God had come upon them. Jesus' presence was the kingdom of God among them. Jesus then refers to the man from whom He had cast out the demon and warned that one must fortify himself with a strong spiritual presence, the Holy Spirit of God, to keep unclean spirits from returning and causing greater havoc in one's life.

Since our culture is not based on shame/honor,
how do we deny the power of God?

Decapolis' Deaf Guy

Healing a Deaf Mute in Decapolis
Based on Mark 7:31-37

Again He went out from the region of Tyre, and came through Sidon to the Sea of Galilee, within the region of Decapolis. They brought to Him one who was deaf and spoke with difficulty, and they implored Him to lay His hand on him. Jesus took him aside from the crowd, by himself, and put His fingers into his ears, and after spitting, He touched his tongue *with the saliva;* and looking up to heaven with a deep sigh, He said to him, "Ephphatha!" that is, "Be opened!" And his ears were opened, and the impediment of his tongue was removed, and he *began* speaking plainly. And He gave them orders not to tell anyone; but the more He ordered them, the more widely they continued to proclaim it. They were utterly astonished, saying, "He has done all things well; He makes even the deaf to hear and the mute to speak." Mark 7:31-37.

This healing took place between the healing of the Canaanite woman's daughter near Sidon (little dogs and table crumbs) and the feeding of 4,000 Gentiles. From the area of Sidon, Jesus and His disciples went to the sea to cross to the area called Decapolis, meaning 10 cities, a Gentile area on the south-east of the Sea of Galilee. The last time Jesus was in this area, He had caused quite a commotion by healing the demoniac who had requested to go with Him when the inhabitants asked Jesus to leave. Jesus told him to go back to his people and tell them how the God of heaven had shown mercy to him that day. Apparently, he had done a good job of spreading the news about Jesus.

Acknowledging God

Upon Jesus' arrival, the people brought a deaf man who also had difficulty speaking. They requested that Jesus put His hands on the man and heal him. Touching implies the transference of vitality, health, and life.

Jesus began by removing the man from the crowd so that he could concentrate on what Jesus was doing. The *Bible Knowledge Commentary*[*] suggests that Jesus' actions were to convey what He planned to do to bring about the healing that had been requested. This could explain the unusual steps that Jesus took to bring about healing: looking to heaven, touching the man's ears, spitting on the ground, touching the man's tongue with His own saliva, looking toward heaven, giving a deep sigh. He then commanded "Be opened" in Aramaic, which was a common language in that area for both Jews and Gentiles.

The man could hear and began to speak plainly! Jesus then told the crowd not to tell anyone about the healing, perhaps to keep down the miracle-seeking crowds that could arise. Imagine—suddenly having the ability to hear and speak and being told not to tell anyone! Humanly speaking, that is a very tough challenge for all of us. However, knowing that God knows best, we are reminded that obedience is greater than sacrifice (1 Samuel 15:22).

Mark notes that a large crowd of mostly Gentiles gathered to hear Jesus' words, which led to a concern about feeding the large group. This led to the feeding of the 4,000 that comes next in the book of Mark.

Despite having the correct biblical answer above, what would you do if you were suddenly given the ability to speak and were told not to tell anyone?

---

[*] *Bible Knowledge Commentary: Old and New Testament,* by Roy Zuck and John Walvoord; David C. Cook, publisher © 1989.

Crying "Messiah" from His Darkness

The Healing of Blind Bartimaeus

Based on Matthew 20:29-34; Mark 10:46-52; Luke 18:35-43

Then they came to Jericho. And as He was leaving Jericho with His disciples and a large crowd, a blind beggar *named* Bartimaeus, the son of Timaeus, was sitting by the road. When he heard that it was Jesus the Nazarene, he began to cry out and say, "Jesus, Son of David, have mercy on me!" Many were sternly telling him to be quiet, but he kept crying out all the more, "Son of David, have mercy on me!" And Jesus stopped and said, "Call him *here.*" So they called the blind man, saying to him, "Take courage, stand up! He is calling for you." Throwing aside his cloak, he jumped up and came to Jesus. And answering him, Jesus said, "What do you want Me to do for you?" And the blind man said to Him, "Rabboni, *I want* to regain my sight!" And Jesus said to him, "Go; your faith has made you well." Immediately he regained his sight and began following Him on the road. Mark 10:46-52.

Reading all three versions of this story in the gospels could lead one to consider the Bible confusing. It is interesting to read how the experts dance around the number of people involved and the circumstances surrounding the healing. Were there one or two blind men healed? And, were they healed as Jesus was entering or leaving Jericho?

If there were two blind men, one of them aggressively took the lead to the point that he is named—Bartimaeus. As to whether Jesus was entering or leaving Jericho, Charles Ryrie* suggested that there

---

* Charles Ryrie is the author of the *Ryrie Study Bible*, Moody Press © 1995.

were two Jerichos—the original where the walls came tumbling down, and a new Jericho built by Herod for his winter palace. Technically, one could have been leaving old Jericho and entering new Jericho at the same time, as they were located just one mile apart.

As Jesus was nearing one of the Jerichos, there was a blind man sitting by the roadside begging. As the crowd approached, he asked what the commotion was and was told that it was Jesus of Nazareth. He had heard of Jesus and began to cry out in his best beggar's voice, calling Him the Son of David, a messianic title, and begging for mercy. The crowd responded by trying to quiet him, perhaps because he was an annoying beggar, or perhaps they did not like his use of a messianic title for Jesus. Bartimaeus responded by yelling even louder, repeating his request.

Jesus responded by calling Bartimaeus to come to Him, which he gladly did, casting off his beggar's garb in the process. Jesus then asked an unusual question of him, "What do you want Me to do for you?" This question was to establish the man's faith in Jesus and to acknowledge his own inability to accomplish this task. This is why we pray even though the Father already knows what we need. Bartimaeus replied, referring to Jesus as his personal Rabbi and requesting to have his sight restored. Jesus responded that the man's faith in Him was the basis for his sight being restored. Bartimaeus solidified his dedication to Jesus by joining His followers, which may account for his name being known.

Most commentators believe that Bartimaeus represents the Jewish population, blind at the side of the road, shrouded in their ignorance and unwilling to accept the restored sight that the Savior was offering. When Bartimaeus was called by Jesus, he threw off his beggar's garment, knowing that he would have a changed life by acknowledging God.

Are you willing to cast off your beggar's garments
and accept new life in Jesus?

Freeing a Stooped Woman

Healing a Crippled Woman on the Sabbath

Based on Luk 13:10-17

And He was teaching in one of the synagogues on the Sabbath. And there was a woman who for eighteen years had had a sickness caused by a spirit; and she was bent double, and could not straighten up at all. When Jesus saw her, He called her over and said to her, "Woman, you are freed from your sickness." And He laid His hands on her; and immediately she was made erect again and *began* glorifying God. But the synagogue official, indignant because Jesus had healed on the Sabbath, *began* saying to the crowd in response, "There are six days in which work should be done; so come during them and get healed, and not on the Sabbath day." But the Lord answered him and said, "You hypocrites, does not each of you on the Sabbath untie his ox or his donkey from the stall and lead him away to water *him?* And this woman, a daughter of Abraham as she is, whom Satan has bound for eighteen long years, should she not have been released from this bond on the Sabbath day?" As He said this, all His opponents were being humiliated; and the entire crowd was rejoicing over all the glorious things being done by Him. Luke 13:10-17.

Jesus was teaching in one of the synagogues when He noticed a crippled woman who was unable to stand erect. Calling her to Himself, Jesus told her, "Woman, you are freed from your sickness." Immediately, she was able to stand erect, overcoming the spirit that had plagued her for 18 years. It is interesting that the spirit that plagued her is not called a demon, suggesting that the illness permeated her existence to the point that she had a spirit of illness about her. She exhibited the proper response by praising God for what had happened to her. The crowd around her began to share in her gratitude, praising God with her.

However, not everyone present was joyous. A synagogue official determined that healing was not a proper Sabbath activity and advised the people to seek healing on the other six days of the week. This pronouncement against healing is not biblical, but one of the many burdens placed on the Sabbath by the religious leaders.

Jesus referred to the religious leaders as hypocrites (see Mark 11:52). The Greek word used here is *hypokrites,* meaning an actor or performer. Actors would often play multiple parts in performances and would hold different masks in front of their faces to speak the lines of particular characters. They would alternate the masks when they changed the character. Our meaning here is "something that is not as it appears."

Jesus pointed out their hypocritical attitude by noting that they would loosen one of their work animals on the Sabbath and permit it to drink water. Jesus pointed out that the woman, a daughter of Abraham, was more valuable in God's sight than an animal and deserved to be freed. Those present in the synagogue agreed with Jesus' words and continued to join the woman in grateful praise to God.

Just as the blind man in a previous study, the woman can also represent the Jewish people bound by spiritual unbelief. Unlike the woman and the blind man, the religious leaders refused to come to Jesus, to be brought into the light, and released from their self-imposed spiritual bondage.

What is binding you from standing erect for Jesus?

The Man Who Saw Walking Trees

Healing a Blind Man at Bethsaida
Based on Mark 8:22-26

And they came to Bethsaida. And they brought a blind man to Jesus and implored Him to touch him. Taking the blind man by the hand, He brought him out of the village; and after spitting on his eyes and laying His hands on him, He asked him, "Do you see anything?" And he looked up and said, "I see men, for I see *them* like trees, walking around." Then again He laid His hands on his eyes; and he looked intently and was restored, and *began* to see everything clearly. And He sent him to his home, saying, "Do not even enter the village." Mark 8:22-26.

Just prior to this miracle in Mark's gospel, Jesus had warned His disciples about the leaven of the Pharisees. Leaven is often used to indicate an unseen influence on people that makes them resistant to Jesus' teachings. The disciples thought Jesus was talking about not having bread with them. Jesus reminded them of the two large groups of people who had been fed and the quanity of pieces of bread collected after everyone had eaten. This was to affirm that Jesus was sufficient for all the bread problems they might face. He expressed His disappointment that they did not yet understand His mission.

As Jesus and His disciples entered the village of Bethsaida, local people, aware of who Jesus was, brought a blind man to Him and implored Him to touch the man with His hands. Remember, touch indicates the transfer of vitality, healing, or life.

Jesus led the man out of the village to avoid the many distractions of the village, including crowds of witnesses. It is interesting that the faith of the recipient was never discussed, and yet faith is a vital part of all healing situations.

Jesus applied spittle and touch to the man's eyes, both being applications used by healers. Jesus then asked the man, "Do you see anything?" The man looked up and said he saw men, but they looked like trees walking around. This probably means that what he saw lacked definition sufficient to identify it. Jesus touched his eyes again, and this time his vision began to clear.

This being the only two-staged healing recorded in Mark may indicate the need to fortify the previously unmentioned faith. His faith was increased as his vision improved, and he ended up seeing clearly and being clearly faithful.

Jesus always met people where they were spiritually. He employed the healing applications that the recipients would expect a healer to use. This is the third time Jesus employed spittle, commonly thought to possess healing powers when from a prophet. Although Jesus met people where they were spiritually, He loved them too much to leave them there.

Jesus completed this miracle by telling the man not to re-enter the village, suggesting that the man did not live there. This seems to support the idea of not telling others about the miracle right away.

Blindness is often used to describe people who do not yet understand what Jesus is trying to teach them. Some believe that this is why Mark included this story right after the disciples seemed to be blind to Jesus' true mission.

> Imagine being able to see all things clearly! Is it possible you don't see as clearly as you think you do?

Lord of the Sabbath

Healing a Man with a Shriveled Hand
Based on Matthew 12:9-13; Mark 3:1-5; Luke 6:6-11

On another Sabbath He entered the synagogue and was teaching; and there was a man there whose right hand was withered. The scribes and the Pharisees were watching Him closely to see if He healed on the Sabbath, so that they might find *reason* to accuse Him. But He knew what they were thinking, and He said to the man with the withered hand, "Get up and come forward!" And he got up and came forward. And Jesus said to them, "I ask you, is it lawful to do good or to do harm on the Sabbath, to save a life or to destroy it?" After looking around at them all, He said to him, "Stretch out your hand!" And he did so; and his hand was restored. But they themselves were filled with rage, and discussed together what they might do to Jesus. Luke 6:6-11.

This healing appears in a series of challenges from religious leaders about Jesus' activities on the Sabbath. Before this healing, Jesus' disciples had picked grain heads as they passed through a field. Rubbing the heads between their hands to separate the chaff from the grain heads, they had eaten the grain. This practice was approved in Leviticus 23:25, permitting people to pick grain in a field as they passed through, but not to collect quantities (like harvesting). The Jewish religious leaders classified the rubbing of the grain between the hands as threshing, which was not allowed on the Sabbath.

Radio preacher and Bible commentator John McArthur* recently

---

* John McArthur is pastor of Grace Community Church in Sun Valley, CA.

revealed that the Jews had created a law to correspond with every letter of the Hebrew Ten Commandments. This was man's attempt to improve on God's law and is why they had so many, often petty, laws (called traditions). Jesus often found Himself at odds with the religious leaders over their traditions.

In this healing miracle Jesus was again in the synagogue teaching on the Sabbath day. There was a man present who had a withered hand. Jesus determined to challenge the religious leaders about their traditions that made the Sabbath a burden. The healing was incidental to the teaching as Jesus attempted to enlighten the religious rulers. This may be why the faith of the recipient was not discussed.

After calling the man to Him, Jesus asked the Pharisees if it was lawful to do good on the Sabbath or to do harm, and to give life or to kill. Jesus looked intently at all the Pharisees and scribes present, offering them an opportunity to answer His question. Mark indicates that Jesus was angry because of their hard-hearted lack of compassion and their lack of response, knowing that their response to the question would support Him doing a healing that Sabbath. This is why they did not answer. They were watching to see if He would heal the man so they might have reason to accuse Him of breaking THEIR Sabbath laws.

Jesus told the man to stretch out his hand, and as he did, his hand was restored.

According to Luke, Jesus' overt disregard for the Pharisees' highly regarded traditions caused them to feel great rage toward Him. This so enraged the Pharisees that they went out and plotted how to destroy Him—even meeting with the Herodians, Jews that wanted to remain under Roman rule.

This section of Scripture shows how Jesus and the Pharisees would remain opposed to each other during His ministry. Their lack of belief in Jesus and their protection of their traditions led them to eventually kill Him.

Lord of the Sabbath

Are there man-made traditions today that lead us to drift from the Savior?

This page intentionally left blank.

Continuity of Mission

Healing a Man with Dropsy
Based on Luke 14:1-6

It happened that when He went into the house of one of the leaders of the Pharisees on *the* Sabbath to eat bread, they were watching Him closely. And there in front of Him was a man suffering from dropsy. And Jesus answered and spoke to the lawyers and Pharisees, saying, "Is it lawful to heal on the Sabbath, or not?" But they kept silent. And He took hold of him and healed him, and sent him away. And He said to them, "Which one of you will have a son or an ox fall into a well, and will not immediately pull him out on a Sabbath day?" And they could make no reply to this. Luke 14:1-6.

Jesus was invited to the home of a Pharisee for bread on a Sabbath day. It is doubtful that this Pharisee was a believer, for the other Pharisees who were guests were watching Jesus to see what He would do on the Sabbath day. A man was there who had dropsy, a condition of the body in which fluids are retained (now called edema), often caused by other disease processes. As the Pharisees considered sicknesses or disabilities the result of their sins, it seems unusual that a man with an obvious illness would be invited to a Pharisee's home. He may have been brought as a test for Jesus, as the Pharisees were gathering "offenses" against Him.

With the man directly before Him, Jesus asked the crowd if it was lawful to heal a man on the Sabbath. The crowd remained silent, not because they were awed by His question, but because they knew the Pharisees were also watching to see if anyone lined up with Jesus.

Jesus touched the man and healed him, and then sent the man away. We do not know if "away" was just somewhere not near Jesus, or whether He sent him to his home, knowing that he had just been there as a test for Him.

In defense of His action of healing the man on the Sabbath, Jesus asked the crowd if anyone who had a son or an ox that fell into a well on the Sabbath day would not make all effort to pull the child or the ox out of the pit. What they considered a well was probably a cistern, a pit with tile-lined walls to hold water during the rainy season for use during a dry season. Jesus' defense of His healing of this man was similar to the logical defense He offered after healing the stooped woman in the synagogue (Luke 13:10-17).

It is interesting that Christ's ministry of teaching and healing was not limited to synagogues but occurred wherever Jesus was. What a stunning example of His dedication to His mission. In the previous chapter, when the Pharisees had told Jesus that Herod was trying to kill Him, trying to influence Him to leave the area, Jesus replied that He had a mission and He would continue His mission every day until it was complete.

What is your Godly mission, and how dedicated are you to its continuance and completion?

Under the Father's Will

The Death of Lazarus
Based on John 11:1-16

Now a certain man was sick, Lazarus of Bethany, the village of Mary and her sister Martha. It was the Mary who anointed the Lord with ointment, and wiped His feet with her hair, whose brother Lazarus was sick. So the sisters sent *word* to Him, saying, "Lord, behold, he whom You love is sick." But when Jesus heard *this,* He said, "This sickness is not to end in death, but for the glory of God, so that the Son of God may be glorified by it." Now Jesus loved Martha and her sister and Lazarus. So when He heard that he was sick, He then stayed two days *longer* in the place where He was. Then after this He said to the disciples, "Let us go to Judea again." The disciples said to Him, "Rabbi, the Jews were just now seeking to stone You, and are You going there again?" Jesus answered, "Are there not twelve hours in the day? If anyone walks in the day, he does not stumble, because he sees the light of this world. But if anyone walks in the night, he stumbles, because the light is not in him." This He said, and after that He said to them, "Our friend Lazarus has fallen asleep; but I go, so that I may awaken him out of sleep." The disciples then said to Him, "Lord, if he has fallen asleep, he will recover." Now Jesus had spoken of his death, but they thought that He was speaking of literal sleep. So Jesus then said to them plainly, "Lazarus is dead, and I am glad for your sakes that I was not there, so that you may believe; but let us go to him." Therefore Thomas, who is called Didymus, said to *his* fellow disciples, "Let us also go, so that we may die with Him." John 11:1-16.

Due to the length of this story and yet the wealth of information, it has been divided into two sections. The first deals with Jesus receiving the notice of Lazarus' illness and discussions with His disciples. The second section deals with Jesus at the tomb.

Jesus received the message that His friend Lazarus was very sick, but He elected to stay an additional two days where He was before starting on the trip to Bethany. This town was located two miles from Jerusalem, and He had been threatened with stoning by Jews in Judea. When His disciples reminded Him of these threats, Jesus remarked that there were only a few hours of daylight in which to do His work. Jesus was committed to His Father's plan and did not fear for Himself while He was in the Father's will.

Jesus used the word "sleep" to describe Lazarus' condition. The disciples thought He was speaking of physical rest and noted that he would awaken from that. (Their confusion is obvious in the Greek, for three different words are translated sleep, and they range from physical rest to spiritual inactivity.)* Jesus then explained in terms they could not misunderstand, "Lazarus is dead." Most commentators believe that Jesus spoke of death as sleep because death was not the final stage of this encounter, as Jesus intended to awaken him to live again. This was similar to His description of Jairus' daughter, whom He had resurrected. This encounter was different from both the little girl and the resurrection of the son of the widow of Nain, as both of these restorations occurred within one day.

Jesus' unusual remark to His disciples that He was glad for their sake He had not gone to Bethany before now indicates that Jesus knew His disciples needed to witness this resurrection to fortify their faith for the coming events. They needed to know that the power of God can resurrect a person after four days, as Jesus had unsuccessfully been trying to tell them that He would die and be resurrected after three days.

Thomas' brave exhortation to the other disciples was just bravado, as no one was coming forward to die with Jesus.

---

* *The New Strong's Exhaustive Concordance of the Bible,* Thomas Nelson Publishing © 2007.

Under the Father's Will

Do you understand the significance of the disciples witnessing this resurrection? If you were a disciple present with Jesus at this time, would you be advising Him not to go to Judah, or joining Thomas in brave—but empty—comments?

This page intentionally left blank.

Lazarus, Come Forth

The Resurrection of Lazarus
Based o John 11:17-44

So when Jesus came, He found that he had already been in the tomb four days. Now Bethany was near Jerusalem, about two miles off; and many of the Jews had come to Martha and Mary, to console them concerning *their* brother. Martha therefore, when she heard that Jesus was coming, went to meet Him, but Mary stayed at the house. Martha then said to Jesus, "Lord, if You had been here, my brother would not have died. Even now I know that whatever You ask of God, God will give You." Jesus said to her, "Your brother will rise again." Martha said to Him, "I know that he will rise again in the resurrection on the last day." Jesus said to her, "I am the resurrection and the life; he who believes in Me will live even if he dies, and everyone who lives and believes in Me will never die. Do you believe this?" She said to Him, "Yes, Lord; I have believed that You are the Christ, the Son of God, *even* He who comes into the world."

When she had said this, she went away and called Mary her sister, saying secretly, "The Teacher is here and is calling for you." And when she heard it, she got up quickly and was coming to Him.

Now Jesus had not yet come into the village, but was still in the place where Martha met Him. Then the Jews who were with her in the house, and consoling her, when they saw that Mary got up quickly and went out, they followed her, supposing that she was going to the tomb to weep there. Therefore, when Mary came where Jesus was, she saw Him, and fell at His feet, saying to Him, "Lord, if You had been here, my brother would not have died." When Jesus therefore saw her weeping, and the Jews who came with her *also* weeping, He was deeply moved in spirit and was troubled, and said, "Where have you laid him?" They said to Him, "Lord, come and see." Jesus wept. So the Jews were saying, "See how He loved him!" But some of them said, "Could not this man, who opened the eyes of the blind

man, have kept this man also from dying?" So Jesus, again being deeply moved within, came to the tomb. Now it was a cave, and a stone was lying against it. Jesus said, "Remove the stone." Martha, the sister of the deceased, said to Him, "Lord, by this time there will be a stench, for he has been *dead* four days." Jesus said to her, "Did I not say to you that if you believe, you will see the glory of God?" So they removed the stone. Then Jesus raised His eyes, and said, "Father, I thank You that You have heard Me. I knew that You always hear Me; but because of the people standing around I said it, so that they may believe that You sent Me." When He had said these things, He cried out with a loud voice, "Lazarus, come forth." The man who had died came forth, bound hand and foot with wrappings, and his face was wrapped around with a cloth. Jesus said to them, "Unbind him, and let him go."
John 11:17-44.

After waiting two days, Jesus and His disciples made the one-day journey to Bethany and found that Lazarus had been dead four days. This means he was already dead when Jesus had received the message of his illness.

Hearing that Jesus was coming, Martha went out to meet Him outside the village and greeted Him with her strong faith in who He was and what He could do. Her faith included His ability to heal, His close connection with the Father, and that God would grant Jesus whatever He requested. She then used three ways of identifying Jesus as Messiah, but she was unaware of His plans.

When Jesus told her that her brother would rise up, she did not expect an immediate resurrection, but agreed that he would rise up like all believers when Jesus comes in the last days. Jesus then identified Himself as the Resurrection and the Life. This is the fifth of seven "I Am" statements of Jesus that often reflect the very thing that He would be doing.

Martha then went to the house and told Mary that the Rabbi was waiting to talk to her. As she got up to go out to meet Him, some of the mourners, many who were from Jerusalem, followed her, believing that she was going to grieve by the tomb.

Mary affirmed her faith in Jesus just as her sister had done. While her faith was just as strong, she also did not expect an immediate resurrection of her brother. The human side of Jesus was grieving over the lost condition of mankind and how death brings people such sorrow. When He asked where they had laid their brother, Mary said, "Come and see."

The mourners and other witnesses, observing Jesus' tears, were still divided on how much He must have loved Lazarus and could He not have come earlier and healed him?

Upon reaching the tomb, Jesus said, "Remove the stone." The family could have denied opening the tomb, but they trusted Jesus even though they did not understand what He was going to do. When Martha protested that the body would surely stink by now, Jesus told her to watch the glory of God.

Jesus then had a talk with His Father, in which He thanked God for hearing Him all the time and for giving Him what He requested. He also said that mentioning His relationship with the Father was to validate that God had indeed sent Him.

Next, Jesus said in a loud voice, "Lazarus, come forth!" Many believe that using the name, Lazarus, limited how many would respond to Jesus' call to resurrection. Although most believe that the "Come forth" referred to him leaving the tomb, it may have been an order to come forth from among the dead. When the man, bound in wrappings, came out of the tomb, Jesus ordered them to release him from the grave clothes, because he would not need them any longer.

Acknowledging God

Can you imagine the great celebration that occurred? Many people believed in Jesus because of this incredible miracle, but there were also some who went to the Pharisees about what had happened (John 11:45, 46). Many people relied on the Jewish leaders to interpret matters for them, and to have witnessed such a miraculous event caused them to question the Pharisees' accusations against Jesus. If you read on, you will find that the religious leaders determined that if they did not stop Jesus, a sharp division among the people would occur, and the Roman leaders would come and take away their place and their nation. Some believed that the place that would be taken away was the temple, but others believed that it was their place in Jewish society that they feared losing—their power, their prestige, their position, and their honor.

What do you fear losing, and what do you stand to lose by holding onto it?

Application

Praise

Almost 20 years ago, during a period I call the year of the medical mishap, I found myself focused inwardly dealing with disabilities. While stumbling past a television, my attention was drawn to a preacher talking about how to remove your focus from yourself and place it on God where it belongs. The speaker was Michael Youssef, an Egyptian-born Christian now living in Atlanta, Georgia, on a program called *Leading the Way.* This sermon was one in a series that became a book called *Empowered by Praise.*[*] By choosing one of God's characteristics and praising Him for that, your relationship with God becomes closer and more personal, and you gain the power of a closer walk with God. I chose God's holiness and began searching the Scriptures for verses pertaining to God's holiness. Through this process, I was able to place God back in the center of my thinking and began to grow in my faith and relationship with Him. By praising God, I became better prepared to serve His people. By praising, God we are reminded of His position in our life, that He is God, and we are not. Think of the characteristics of God, choose one, and begin to search His Word to know Him better.

Two years ago, in a small church in the Florida Keys, the subject of praising God came up during a Sabbath School class. A member

---

[*] Michael Youssef, *Empowered by Praise: How God Responds When You Revel in His Glory,* Kobri Publishing © 2011.

questioned how we could praise God when so many things were going wrong. He then listed a few, including repairs to his vehicle.

A visitor pointed out that we praise God for who He is and what He has done for us, not based on our current situation. The visitor continued by saying, "Would I give up my vision if I could see God? Would I give up my hearing if I could hear God's call on my life? Would I give up my mobility if I could walk closer to God? If the answer to these questions is yes, then your relationship with God is correct." The member stood up and declared that the Spirit of God was surely with us all that day.

> If you interrogate your circumstances, do they define your relationship with God?

Worship

Occasionally I would ask a group to define worship, and they would usually answer with activities like hymns, mission stories, sermons, and prayer. After acknowledging the usefulness of these activities, I would suggest that worship is something that happens between you and God—a connection. Worship may occur when you are engaged in the activities listed above, but it is not limited to those activities.

Application

How do you connect with God to experience true worship?

One of my favorite Old Testament stories is found in Ezekiel 37, where the prophet is shown a valley of dry bones, and God asks, "Will these bones live again?" The prophet answers, "You know, Lord." There is then a rattling of the bones in the valley, and they come together, and muscle and sinew and tendons form on the bones. They look like men, but they are not alive. God then tells the prophet to call the wind to enter the bodies. The Hebrew word *rauch* and the Greek word *pneumo* both refer to wind, breath, or spirit. After Ezekiel calls the *rauch,* it enters the bodies, and they become alive.

Although this was a metaphor about reviving the nation Israel, I believe it also applies to us as believers today. If you really want to be alive, you need *rauch,* the Spirit. Although you receive the Spirit as a gift from God when you accept what Christ has done for you and know He is the Son of God, you must submit yourself to the Spirit's leading to gain the full benefit. "For who among people knows the *thoughts* of a person except the spirit of the person that is in him? So also the *thoughts* of God no one knows, except the Spirit of God." 1 Corinthians 2:11. The Spirit that dwells in us and knows the mind of God makes the spiritual connection that welds our minds to His will, and we experience true worship.

The Spirit also leads us into serving God's people. Author Kim Meeder[*] describes the Holy Spirit as a raging river, which no man can tell where to go. She suggests that you jump in (I would recommend a boat) and see where the river takes you. For wherever the Holy Spirit takes you, He will prepare you for that destination and the service that you are to perform there.

Do you appreciate the Holy Spirit as a raging river, and do you see yourself as a conduit of the Spirit?

---

[*] Kim Meeder, *Encountering Our Wild God: Ways to Experience His Untamable Presence Every Day,* Baker Publishing Group © 2018.

Service

Based on John 6:1-14

After these things Jesus went away to the other side of the Sea of Galilee (or Tiberias). A large crowd followed Him, because they saw the signs which He was performing on those who were sick. Then Jesus went up on the mountain, and there He sat down with His disciples. Now the Passover, the feast of the Jews, was near. Therefore Jesus, lifting up His eyes and seeing that a large crowd was coming to Him, said to Philip, "Where are we to buy bread, so that these may eat?" This He was saying to test him, for He Himself knew what He was intending to do. Philip answered Him, "Two hundred denarii worth of bread is not sufficient for them, for everyone to receive a little." One of His disciples, Andrew, Simon Peter's brother, said to Him, "There is a lad here who has five barley loaves and two fish, but what are these for so many people?" Jesus said, "Have the people sit down." Now there was much grass in the place. So the men sat down, in number about five thousand. Jesus then took the loaves, and having given thanks, He distributed to those who were seated; likewise also of the fish as much as they wanted. When they were filled, He said to His disciples, "Gather up the leftover fragments so that nothing will be lost." So they gathered them up, and filled twelve baskets with fragments from the five barley loaves which were left over by those who had eaten. Therefore when the people saw the sign which He had performed, they said, "This is truly the Prophet who is to come into the world." John 6:1-14.

The feeding of the 5,000 is not only a great miracle, but it also teaches us Jesus' plan for drawing us into service.

Application

The first thing Jesus did was to establish that feeding the large group was beyond human means, so when it happened it must have been a miracle, and praise was due to God.

Jesus then asked the disciples to make an inventory and bring it to Him. Jesus then blessed what they had found and returned it to them to distribute to the people.

We notice that the disciples did recognize the problem: the masses needed to be fed. People that are Spirit-led will see many needs that require attention. Imagine what must have gone through the minds of the disciples as they continued to distribute what had originally been two little fish and five little biscuits! And of course, there were baskets of leftovers after everyone had eaten their fill. This was another reminder of the miraculous work that had just been done.

Today, as we recognize a need within the church or the community, we come to God with our inventory of skills and talents. When God blesses what we have provided, He returns it to us to distribute to those in need. God always blesses the masses through His followers. If you are Spirit led, you are in the process of service to God's people.*

Knowing that Jesus calls us to be lights to the world, yet many of us feel our lights are only like a 5-watt bulb—a nightlight. However, in the darkest part of the night a 5-watt bulb can show us the way. So, as our world grows darker, even a 5-watt bulb can illuminate the way to Jesus.

So where are you in this process: recognizing a need, making an inventory, bringing it to Jesus to bless, distributing to those in need, or collecting the bounty of leftovers?

* For a modern-day account of Spirit leading and healing, see Kim Meeder's book *Encountering Our Wild God,* © 2018, Chosen, a division of Baker Publishing Group, Minneapolis, MN. This inspirational book reveals how a modern Spirit-led person's life involves the miraculous hand of God.

This page intentionally left blank.

This page intentionally left blank.

This page intentionally left blank.

This page intentionally left blank.

This page intentionally left blank.

This page intentionally left blank.

This page intentionally left blank.

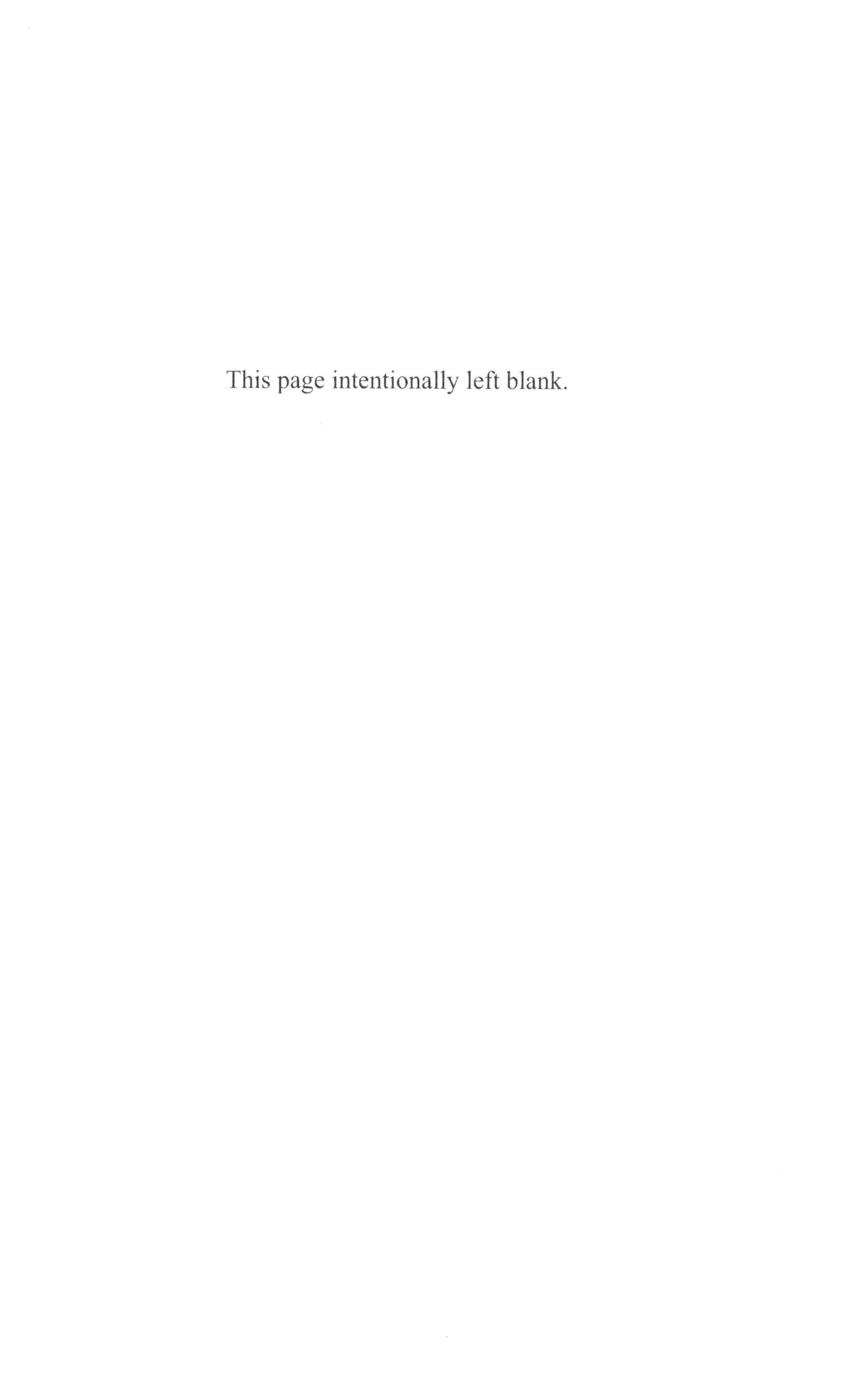

This page intentionally left blank.

This page intentionally left blank.

Made in the USA
Middletown, DE
29 November 2021